ADVENTURES WITH ATOMS AND MOLECULES

BOOK V

CHEMISTRY EXPERIMENTS FOR YOUNG PEOPLE

— Adventures with Science —

ROBERT C. MEBANE

THOMAS R. RYBOLT

ENSLOW PUBLISHERS, INC.

44 Fadem Road	P.O. Box 38
Box 699	Aldershot
Springfield, N.J. 07081	Hants GU12 6BP
U.S.A.	U.K.

ACKNOWLEDGMENT

We wish to thank Mickey Sarquis of Miami University, Ohio; Ron Perkins of Greenwich High School, Connecticut; and Dr. Clarence Murphy of East Stroudsburg University, Pennsylvania; for reviewing the manuscript.

DEDICATION

For the memory of Bob Pierotti —TR
For Ben Gross —RM, TR

Library of Congress Cataloging-in-Publication Data
(Revised for volume 5)

Mebane, Robert C.
    Adventures with atoms and molecules.

    Includes indexes.
    Chemistry experiments for home or school demonstrate the properties and behavior of various kinds of atoms and molecules.
        1. Chemistry—Experiments—Juvenile literature.
        2. Chemistry—Experiments. 3. Molecules—Experiments.
        4. Experiments. I. Rybolt, Thomas R.
QD38.M43   1985   540'.78   85-10177
ISBN   0-89490-120-6   (v.   1)
ISBN   0-89490-164-8   (v.   2)
ISBN   0-89490-254-7   (v.   3)
ISBN   0-89490-336-5   (v.   4)
ISBN   0-89490-606-2   (v.   5)

Printed in the United States of America

10 9 8 7 6 5 4 3 2

Illustration Credit: Kimberly Austin Daly

CONTENTS

FOREWORD

This is the fifth in a series of books of hands-on science experiments for young people. The authors, Thomas R. Rybolt and Robert C. Mebane, begin each activity by posing an interesting question. Which evaporates faster, diet or regular cola? Does the top or bottom of a wet paper towel dry quicker? What happens when grapes are placed in water? The answers are found by experimenting with readily available household materials.

Each of the activities is carefully written to include a safe procedure, an explanation of the phenomena, and interesting ideas for other things to try. The activities encourage young people in upper elementary and middle schools to better observe and understand their world. They will learn how to generate a radio wave with an electric light switch; how to make bleach from salt water; and how to test for iron in water with tea. They will understand better the molecular explanation of why cutting onions brings tears to your eyes and why heat smooths wrinkled clothing.

This series is a wealth of ideas for home experimentation or school science fair projects. With the addition of *Book V* in this series, young people now can choose from 150 interesting science experiments. The "Other things to try" sections at the end of each activity provide several hundred additional ideas for open-ended experiments.

The authors continue to encourage young people to study the science of everyday things!

Ronald I. Perkins
Assistant Director
Institute for Chemical Education
University of Wisconsin—Madison

4

INTRODUCTION

SCIENCE

Science is an adventure! Science is an adventure of asking questions and finding answers. Scientists are men and women who ask questions. Scientists answer questions by doing experiments and making observations. The results of their observations increase our knowledge and improve our understanding of the world around us.

Science is exciting because it never stops. There will always be new questions to ask. New questions lead to new experiments. New experiments lead to new knowledge and to new questions.

Experimentation is the heart of science. Experimentation lays the foundation upon which the basic principles of science are understood. You can gain a better feeling as to what science really is by doing and experiencing science.

One way to share in the adventure of science is to do experiments. In our first four books, <u>Adventures With Atoms and Molecules</u>, <u>Adventures With Atoms and Molecules, Book II</u>, <u>Adventures With Atoms and Molecules, Book III</u>, and <u>Adventures With Atoms and Molecules, Book IV</u>, we presented 120 experiments and suggestions for over 240 additional activities. Those books were a start, but there are many more experiments waiting to be done.

This book is a further collection of experiments that you can do at home or at school. These experiments will help you learn how to ask questions and find answers, and how to become a better observer. As you read about science and do experiments, you will learn more about yourself and your world. In asking questions and doing experiments, you will learn that observing and trying to understand the world around you is interesting and fun.

ATOMS, IONS, AND MOLECULES

One of the most important things that scientists have learned about our world is that EVERYTHING IS MADE OF ATOMS. Water, ice, air, sand, table salt, sugar, rocks, shoes, clothes, houses, bicycles, cars, leaves, trees, flowers, bees, ants, spiders, cows, horses, and people are all made of atoms.

Atoms are the basic building blocks of all things. There are ninety-two different kinds of natural atoms. A few additional atoms have been made by scientists in laboratories. Examples of natural atoms include: oxygen, hydrogen, carbon, mercury, gold, silver, helium, chlorine, neon, nickel, iron, phosphorus, and aluminum.

Atoms are found in all things. For example, a piece of aluminum foil is made of aluminum atoms. A diamond consists of carbon atoms. Sand is made of silicon and oxygen atoms. Table sugar is made of carbon, hydrogen, and oxygen atoms.

Molecules are combinations of tightly bound atoms. Water is a combination of hydrogen and oxygen atoms. Imagine you have a drop of water and you divide this drop into smaller and smaller drops. If you could continue to divide the drops enough times, you would eventually end up with a single water molecule. If you divided this water molecule any further, you would have two hydrogen atoms and one oxygen atom.

Scientists use models to represent molecules. Sometimes the models are made from small balls with the balls representing atoms. These models allow scientists to understand more about molecules.

Molecules that are made of only a few atoms are very small. Molecules are so small that you cannot see one even with the most powerful optical microscope. One drop of water contains about two million quadrillion (2,000,000,000,000,000,000,000) molecules. If you took two million quadrillion pennies and stacked one on top of the other, you could make three hundred thousand (300,000) stacks of pennies. Each stack would reach from the Sun to Pluto. Pluto is the planet in our solar system that is the greatest distance from the sun.

If you could magnify one drop of water to the size of the earth, each water molecule would be about the size of an orange.

Polymers are giant molecules made by combining many smaller molecules. Some polymer molecules may contain several million atoms. Important natural polymers include natural rubber, starch, and DNA. Rubber bands and some automobile tires are made of natural rubber. Starch is found in many foods. DNA is the molecule of heredity. Some important polymers made by scientists are nylon, which is used in making fabrics; polyethylene, which is used in making plastic bags and plastic bottles; and polystyrene, which is used in making Styrofoam cups and insulation.

Atoms are made of smaller particles. These smaller particles are electrons, protons, and neutrons. The nucleus is the center of the atom and contains protons and neutrons. Protons are positively charged, and neutrons have no charge. Electrons are negatively charged and are found around the nucleus.

Atoms and molecules that contain a charge are called ions. Ions have either a positive charge or a negative charge. Positive ions have more protons than electrons. Negative ions have more electrons than protons. Sodium chloride, which is the chemical name for table salt, is made of positive sodium ions and negative chlorine ions.

Atoms or ions sometimes combine in chemical reactions to make molecules, metal alloys, or salts. Chemical reactions can also involve changing one molecule into a different molecule or breaking one molecule down into smaller molecules, atoms, or ions.

ABOUT THE EXPERIMENTS IN THIS BOOK

In this book we present thirty experiments and suggestions for more than sixty additional activities. Many of the new experiments will show you how experimentation can be used to understand phenomena you encounter in your everyday life. Have you ever wondered why an onion brings tears to your eyes, why wrinkles disappear when clothes are ironed, or why your hair is more elastic when it's wet? You will find out through some of the experiments in this book.

Each experiment is divided into five parts: 1) materials, 2) procedure, 3) observations, 4) discussion, and 5) other things to try. The materials are what you need to do the experiment. The procedure is what you do. The observations are what you see. The discussion explains what your observations tell you about atoms and molecules. The other things to try are additional questions and experiments that you can do to find out more about atoms and molecules.

This book is intended to be used and not just read. It is a guide toward doing, observing, and thinking science. The experimental activities described in this book are designed to give you an opportunity to experience science.

Do not worry about trying to understand everything about an experiment. You do not have to memorize words or meanings when you are first involved in science. You need to experience science first.

You do not have to do the experiments in the order they appear in the book. Each activity has been written to stand completely alone. You will find that some experiments discuss the same ideas. It will help you learn and understand these ideas to see them more than once.

Not every experiment you do will work the way you expect every time. Something may be different in the experiment when you do it. Repeat the experiment if it gives an unexpected result and think about what may be different.

Not all of the experiments in this book give immediate results. Some experiments in this book will take time to see observable results. Some of the experiments in this book may take a shorter time than that suggested in the experiment. Some experiments may take a longer time than suggested. You must be patient when doing experiments.

The illustrations in this book are not intended to be a photographic or artistic substitution for what you will do and observe. The purpose of these illustrations is to direct your attention to one or two key features of what you may expect to observe when you do each experiment.

SAFETY NOTE

WHEN YOU DO THESE EXPERIMENTS MAKE SURE YOU

1) Obtain an adult's permission before you do these experiments and activities.
2) Get an adult to watch you when you do an experiment. They enjoy seeing experiments too.
3) Follow the specific directions given for each experiment.
4) Clean up after each experiment.

NOTE TO TEACHERS, PARENTS, AND OTHER ADULTS

All of us are born with a natural curiosity regarding the world around us. This intrinsic interest in nature is the motivation for most scientific activity. To avoid a dulling of this interest as children grow older, it is necessary to provide experiences for young people that show the connection of science to everyday life and the world around us.

Science is not merely a collection of facts but a way of thinking. Our series of books—Adventures With Atoms and Molecules— is a tool to help children and young people become actively involved in the process of science. Explanations for each experimental activity are provided for completeness, but the experience of the activity is more important than the explanation. The experience can last a lifetime, and understanding can develop with time.

As teachers, parents, and other adults, you can play a key role in maintaining and encouraging a young person's interest in science. As you do experiments with a young person, you may find your own curiosity being expanded.

Remember, science is for everyone!

The adventure continues . . .

CAN SOLID ICE ABSORB MORE HEAT THAN LIQUID SALT WATER?

1

Materials

Two clear plastic cups	Tablespoon
Water	Permanent marker
Salt	Notebook paper
Outdoor household thermometer	Pen
Refrigerator with freezer	Clock or watch
Measuring cup	

Procedure

Use a permanent marker to write "water" on the first cup. Write "salt water" on the second cup.

Add one cup of water to the first cup. Add one cup of water to the second cup. Add three tablespoons of salt to the second cup, and stir for about one minute. Place the cup of water, cup of salt water, and an outdoor thermometer in a refrigerator freezer. Allow the cups and thermometer to remain in the freezer overnight.

The next day remove both cups and the thermometer. Immediately read the temperature of the thermometer and write down the temperature and the time on a piece of notebook paper. Set both cups on a table or counter where you can leave them undisturbed for several hours.

Wait about two hours and then observe each cup. Record the time on your paper. Then record the temperature of the water and the temperature of the salt water by placing the thermometer in each cup. The salt water should be a liquid. The cup of pure water should be a mixture of solid ice and liquid water. If enough ice is melted you will be able to insert the thermometer in the water. However, if the ice is solid, do not try to force the thermometer into the cup—wait until the ice melts further.

Check the temperature in each cup once every hour for the next three hours. Continue to record the times and the temperatures you observe.

Observations

Does the water or salt water remain colder longer? Which cup warms up faster?

Discussion

You should find that the pure water remains colder longer than the salt water.

A mixture of salt and water requires a lower temperature to freeze than pure water. A refrigerator freezer is cold enough (about -16°C or

4°F) to freeze pure water. However, it is not cold enough to freeze salt water.

After remaining in the freezer overnight, the water is a solid, but the salt water is still a liquid. The salt water may be slushy like a thick liquid, but should not be frozen solid.

At the start of the experiment both the solid water and the liquid salt water are the same temperature. However, as time passes, the salt water warms more quickly than the solid water. The amounts of both are about the same, and the starting temperatures are the same. So why is the pure water slower to warm up than the salt water?

The salt water is warming but is already a liquid. Water is undergoing a change from a solid to a liquid and then warming up. This additional change from a solid to a liquid requires extra energy.

A lot of extra energy is needed to change water from a solid to a liquid. The pure solid water takes longer to warm up because it has to absorb more energy than the salt water before it gets to room temperature.

Other things to try

Some hair curlers have a hollow center filled with wax. When the curlers are heated, the wax melts and changes from a cold solid to a hot liquid. You can shake the hot curler and hear the liquid sloshing inside.

Why would you need a curler center which goes from a liquid to a solid instead of just a solid center? The hot liquid can store more energy than a solid. Extra energy must be put in to change the solid to a liquid. Can a wax-filled curler store more energy than a solid curler?

2

WHAT HAPPENS WHEN FLOATING ICE CUBES TOUCH?

Materials

Ice cubes   Sink
Bowl   Warm water

Procedure

Fill the bowl with slightly warm water from a sink faucet. Set the bowl beside the sink. Place two large ice cubes in the bowl of water. The water should be deep enough so the ice cubes float.

Gently move the ice cubes together so they touch each other. Watch the ice cubes as they touch. Continue to observe the ice cubes. You may need to repeat this experiment several times.

Observations

What happens when the ice cubes first touch? What do you observe happening as the ice cubes melt?

Discussion

You probably observe that the two ice cubes freeze together when they touch. The two ice cubes may combine to form one larger ice cube. Even as the cubes are melting and getting smaller in the warm water, the two cubes remain stuck together.

The behavior of the cubes may not be the same every time you do the experiment. They may remain together for a time, then separate, and then come back together. They may come apart, or they may stay frozen together.

The ice cubes melt because the cold cubes are placed in warm water. Heat moves from the warm water into the colder ice. As the outer surface of an ice cube warms above 0°C (32°F), it changes from a solid to a liquid.

Why do two melting cubes freeze together when they touch? As the cubes come together, there is a thin layer of water between them. Because it is colder than the melting point of ice on both sides of this thin layer, the water changes from a liquid back to a solid. The water between the cubes freezes and locks the cubes together.

The cubes may come apart later or they may stay frozen in one larger piece. The outer parts of the cubes melt first. The area where they freeze together becomes part of the center of a larger cube. If this part is slow to melt, the cubes remain stuck together.

Other things to try

Repeat this experiment using hotter or colder tap water. Do the results change in hotter or colder water?

Repeat this experiment in a larger bowl with three or four ice cubes. Can you get several ice cubes to freeze together to make one large ice cube?

Place one piece of ice on a flat surface. Put a few drops of water on top of this piece of ice. Place another ice cube on top of the first. Do they freeze together?

WHICH EVAPORATES FASTER: OIL OR WATER?

3

Materials
Two clear plastic cups
Water
Cooking oil
Permanent marker
Measuring cup

Procedure
Add one cup of water to the first plastic cup. Add one cup of cooking oil to the second plastic cup. Set both cups indoors where they can remain undisturbed for a week. If the cups are placed in a warm sunny spot, evaporation will occur faster.

Observe the cups after two, four, and six days from the time they were first filled. You can record the level of the liquid in each cup after each observation by marking the level on the outside of the cup.

Observations
How do the levels of the water and oil compare after two, four, and six days? Does oil or water evaporate faster?

Discussion
You should see the water evaporate (go into the air) faster than the oil and to a much greater extent. The water should disappear from the cup while the oil does not. The water is able to evaporate at room temperature. The oil is not able to evaporate easily.

Water is a small molecule made of two hydrogen atoms and one oxygen atom. Water is a polar molecule because there is a positive and a negative side. The positive and negative sides of different water

molecules are attracted to each other. These attractive forces help keep water molecules next to each other in a liquid.

Oil is made of molecules much larger than the water molecules. These oil molecules have some oxygen atoms, but are mostly carbon and hydrogen atoms. Oil molecules are nonpolar because they don't have positive and negative sides.

Because oil molecules are much bigger than water, oil molecules are held together more strongly than water. For this reason oil does not evaporate (go from a liquid to a gas) as quickly as water.

When a liquid changes to a gas, it evaporates. Evaporation is faster at a higher temperature. Heat energy causes some molecules to move fast enough to leave the liquid and go into the air. The temperature of the room is high enough to gradually cause more and more of the water to change from liquid to vapor. The temperature of the room is not high enough to make the oil evaporate and go into the air.

At a high enough temperature, liquids will boil. When a liquid boils, bubbles of vapor form in the liquid. Water boils at 100°C (212°F). Oil boils at a much higher temperature than water. Since oil can be raised to a higher temperature without boiling, oil can be used to cook foods quickly.

Other things to try

Repeat this experiment, but place the cups outside on a hot, sunny day. Observe the level of the liquids in each cup after two, four, and six hours. Does the water evaporate more quickly than the oil? How fast is the evaporation compared to your original experiment?

Place two cups of water outside on a hot, sunny day. Pour enough oil in one of the cups to cover the water with a layer of oil. Observe the level of water in each cup after five hours. How does the layer of oil affect the evaporation of the water? Can you explain your observations?

HOW DO DIET AND REGULAR COLA DIFFER AS THEY EVAPORATE?

4

Materials

Can of diet cola
Can of regular cola
Two plastic cups

Measuring cup
Permanent marker

Procedure

Pour one-half cup of regular cola into one plastic cup. Pour one-half cup of diet cola into the other plastic cup. Mark a "D" on the outside of the diet cola cup so it can be identified.

Set both cups inside where they can remain undisturbed for about two weeks. Observe the cups every other day for the next two weeks. Compare the height of liquid remaining in each cup.

If the cups are placed in a warm, sunny spot, the evaporation will happen faster.

Observations

What happens in each of the cups? Does all the liquid disappear from either of the cups?

Discussion

A diet and regular cola may both taste sweet and look the same. However, as they evaporate, you can tell the difference.

You should observe that the amount of liquid in each cup gradually decreases. After a week or two, you should see that all the liquid is gone from the diet cola cup. However, the regular cola cup should still contain a small amount of liquid. The remaining liquid should be a thick syrup. It should be viscous (slow to pour) like maple syrup.

Regular cola is sweetened by natural sugars such as fructose and sucrose. Diet cola is sweetened by artificial sweeteners such as aspartame (Nutrasweet®).

An artificial sweetener such as aspartame is about 150 times sweeter than the same amount of sucrose. Therefore, it takes a lot of sugar, but only a tiny amount of aspartame to sweeten a cola.

Evaporation causes water to change from a liquid to a gas. Water seems to disappear as it evaporates. The water molecules leave the liquid and go into the air. We cannot see water molecules in the air, but they are there. In the liquid, water molecules are next to each other. In the air, the water molecules are far apart.

A diet or regular cola is mostly carbonated water (carbon dioxide gas dissolved in water). The carbon dioxide gas goes into the air fairly quickly. You see bubbles of gas form and rise to the surface. The water evaporates more slowly and may take days to go into the air.

The sugar in a regular cola causes this beverage to evaporate slower and leave behind a thick syrup of concentrated sugar water. The sugar cannot evaporate and tends to hold some of the water with it. However, the diet cola has only a small amount of sweetener and a few other added ingredients. When a diet cola evaporates, it leaves behind only a small amount of artificial sweetener in the bottom of the cup.

Other things to try

Repeat this experiment using other liquids, such as orange juice, tomato juice, coffee, and tea. Observe how fast they evaporate and what is left behind as the water disappears.

DOES THE TOP OR BOTTOM OF A   **5**
WET PAPER TOWEL DRY QUICKER?

Materials

String (about four feet long)	Two paper clips
Tape	Paper towel
Watch or clock	Water

Procedure

Tape the ends of a piece of string to the wall above a sink. Completely wet the paper towel. Fold one inch of the wet paper towel over the string. Carefully slip a paper clip over each end of the paper towel folded over the string. These paper clips should hold the paper towel on the string. The paper towel should hang above the sink but not touch any surface.

Feel the top and bottom of the towel. The top and bottom should be wet. Let the towel hang for about fifteen minutes and check it again. Feel the top and the bottom. Check the top and bottom of the towel again about five or ten minutes later.

Observations

Does the top or the bottom of the towel dry quicker?

Discussion

You probably observe that the top of the towel dries while the bottom is still wet. The top dries quicker than the bottom.

If you have ever felt clothes or towels drying outside, you may have noticed this difference. Laundry hanging on a clothesline tends to dry quicker at the top and slower at the bottom. Why does the top dry quicker?

You might just think that gravity just pulls all the water to the bottom of a hanging towel or cloth. Gravity pulls water down, but capillaries (small channels) within a material tend to make water spread out. At first, excess water may drip off the bottom of the material. However, gravity cannot pull all the water out of a material.

When water evaporates, it goes from a liquid to a vapor. Water evaporates from the towel. This evaporation cools the towel and a thin layer of air immediately next to the towel.

Cooler air is heavier than warmer air. The cool air next to the towel is heavier than the surrounding air. This heavier air falls along the side of the towel.

As the air moves down beside the towel, it picks up more water from the towel. However, when this thin layer of air becomes saturated (filled) with water, it cannot carry any more. Therefore, more water evaporates at the top than at the bottom of the paper towel. The layer of air passing over the bottom of the towel is already saturated with water and cannot pick up any more. A towel or other hanging material dries from the top down.

Other things to try

Hang a dry paper towel on a string above a sink. Pour some water on the towel. Watch the water spread out on the towel. Does some of the water go down? Does some of the water flow up? How do you explain your observations? Check the towel every ten minutes until it is dry. Which end dries quicker?

DOES A BICYCLE TIRE PUMP   **6**
CHANGE TEMPERATURE DURING USE?

Materials
Bicycle tire pump (push-type, not electric)
Bicycle tire
Air pressure gauge

Procedure
Remove the protective cap from the air valve on the bicycle tire. Press the inner post of the valve to release air from the tire. Release air until the tire is nearly flat. You may find an air gauge useful in releasing the air. Most air gauges have a point on them for releasing air from a tire valve.

Securely attach the bicycle tire pump to the valve on the bicycle tire. To get a sense of the temperature of the pump, feel the tube of the bicycle tire pump about an inch from the bottom of the pump.

Push up and down on the bicycle tire pump to refill the bicycle tire with air. Continue to pump until the tire feels firm. Use the air pressure gauge to make sure you do not overinflate the tire.

After filling the tire with air, check the temperature of the pump by touching the tube of the bicycle tire pump about an inch from the bottom of the pump. Also touch the top of the tube of the bicycle tire pump.

Observations
Is the tube near the bottom of the bicycle tire pump cool or warm before you pump air into the bicycle tire? After pumping, is the bottom of the tube cool or warm? Is the top of the pump tube cool or warm after pumping?

Discussion

A bicycle tire pump consists of a piston and a valve for air delivery. The long tube of the pump is the cylinder of the piston. The piston is attached to the rod that comes out of the top of the long tube and is attached to a handle. Most pistons used in bicycle tire pumps consist of a cup-shaped shaped disc usually made of leather.

When you push down on the pump, air inside the cylinder is compressed. When air is compressed, the molecules in the air are made to move closer together. The pressure inside the cylinder increases.

When the pressure inside the cylinder of the pump becomes greater than the air pressure inside the tire being inflated, the compressed air goes into the tire.

In this experiment, you should find that the tube of the bicycle tire pump near the bottom of the pump becomes warm during pumping. The bottom of the pump cylinder becomes warm because gases become heated when they are compressed. Since the air is compressed at the bottom of the pump, only the bottom of the pump becomes warm. The top of the pump remains cool.

Other things to try

What is the fewest number of times you have to pump up and down to feel heat near the bottom of the pump?

24

IS GRAPHITE SLIPPERY? 7

Materials
Graphite lubricant (available in most hardware stores)
Aluminum foil
Coin (a quarter works well)
Countertop

Procedure
Place a sheet of aluminum foil about the size of notebook paper on a countertop. Place a coin in the center of the foil. While keeping the coin flat on the aluminum foil, try pushing the coin around the aluminum foil.

Remove the coin from the aluminum foil. Lightly squeeze a small amount (about half the size of a pea) of graphite lubricant in the center of the aluminum foil. Graphite lubricant is a very fine powder. Do not use in a windy place or the powder will scatter. Place the coin on top of the graphite. Now try pushing the coin around the aluminum foil.

Observations
Describe the appearance of the graphite lubricant. Is it easier to push the coin around the aluminum foil with or without the graphite lubricant?

Discussion
Graphite is a soft mineral that is mined from the ground. Important graphite mines are found in Canada, Mexico, the Austrian Alps, and on the island of Ceylon. Graphite can also be made from petroleum.

Graphite is made of overlapping layers which contain only carbon atoms. Each carbon atom in a layer of graphite is attached (bonded) to three other carbon atoms. The carbon atoms in a layer of graphite are arranged in a repeating hexagonal pattern—like chicken wire.

The layers of carbon atoms in graphite can slip over each other easily. This makes graphite a good lubricant. Oil and grease are good lubricants too. Graphite has an advantage over oil and grease as a lubricant because it can withstand high temperatures. Oil and grease can break down at high temperatures.

The word graphite comes from the Greek word graphein, which means "to write." Graphite has been used as the "lead" in pencils since the middle of the sixteenth century. Earlier, an alloy of lead metal was actually used in pencils.

Each time you write with a pencil, layers of graphite shear off the end of the pencil and stick to the paper. The layers of graphite shear easily off the tip of a pencil because the layers slip easily over each other.

Graphite is also used in making matches, explosives, shoe polish, steel, and batteries.

Other things to try

Ask an adult if you can add some graphite lubricant to a squeaky door hinge in your house. Does the door hinge stop squeaking?

Can the graphite lubricant make two pieces of wood slide more easily over each other? How can you find out?

CAN OIL KEEP SYRUP FROM STICKING TO METAL?   8

Materials
Two small metal spoons
Cooking oil
Corn syrup
Small bowl

Procedure
Fill one small metal spoon with cooking oil. Pour the oil in the spoon into the small bowl. Now fill the same spoon with corn syrup. Pour the corn syrup from the spoon into the bowl. Observe the spoon carefully as the syrup pours from the spoon.

Fill the second metal spoon with corn syrup. Pour the corn syrup from the spoon into the bowl. Observe the spoon carefully as the syrup pours from the spoon.

Observations
Does the corn syrup pour more easily from the spoon that was coated with oil or from the clean spoon? Does all the corn syrup slide out of the spoon coated with oil? Does all the corn syrup slide out of the clean spoon?

Discussion
You should find that the corn syrup pours more easily from the spoon that was coated with oil. All the corn syrup should slide out of the oil-coated spoon. In contrast, some corn syrup should have stuck to the clean spoon.

Both oil and corn syrup stick to metal spoons. The molecules in oil and the molecules in corn syrup are attracted to the metal surface

of the spoon. This attraction between liquid molecules and a surface is called adhesion.

When you pour the oil out of the spoon, a thin film of oil remains on the spoon because of adhesion. When you add corn syrup to this spoon, the thin film remaining on the spoon keeps the corn syrup from touching the spoon.

The oil and corn syrup do not mix (under normal circumstances). Corn syrup is polar and oil is nonpolar. Polar substances generally do not easily mix with nonpolar substances.

When you pour the corn syrup from the spoon, all the corn syrup in the spoon pours out easily. When you pour corn syrup from the clean spoon some corn syrup sticks to the spoon because of adhesion.

Other things to try

Repeat this experiment with different kinds of cooking oil. How do they compare?

Repeat this experiment with other thick, sticky liquids like molasses and honey. What do you observe?

CAN YOU DETECT AN ELECTRICAL SPARK WITH A RADIO?   9

Materials
Portable radio
Room with light switch

Procedure
Turn on the portable radio and set it to receive AM stations. Tune the radio until you hear just static—not a radio station. Hold the radio near a light switch. While listening to the static coming from the radio, flip the light switch to turn the lights on. Flip the light switch to turn the lights off. Repeat several times.

Observations
What do you hear when you turn on the lights? What do you hear when you turn off the lights?

Discussion
A light switch is used to turn electricity on or off. When a light switch is flipped to turn on a light, the electrical circuit to the light is completed. Electricity flows through the completed circuit and the light glows. When a light switch is flipped to turn a light off, the electrical circuit is disconnected. Electricity stops flowing and the light goes out.

In most light switches, two pieces of metal are brought in contact to complete a circuit. When a circuit is disconnected, the two pieces of metal in the light switch which are in contact with each other are moved apart.

When a switch is flipped to turn on a light, a tiny spark of electricity forms as the two metal pieces in the switch come in contact. A tiny spark of electricity also forms when the two metal pieces in the switch are moved apart to disconnect the light.

The tiny electrical spark that forms when a light switch is flipped on or off generates radio waves. Radio waves are a form of energy.

The radio waves generated by an electrical spark can often be heard on a radio. In this experiment, the sharp cracking sound you hear from your portable radio when you flip a nearby light switch on and off is caused by radio waves generated by an electrical spark in the light switch.

Strong radio waves are generated during lightning storms. These strong radio waves are often heard as crackling static over radios, televisions, and telephones.

Other things to try

Does moving the portable radio farther away from the light switch have an effect on the crackling sound received by the radio when the light switch is flipped?

Repeat this experiment with your radio set to receive FM stations. Do you still hear a sharp crackling sound when you flip a light switch to turn the lights either on or off?

DOES THE COLOR IN A BALLOON **10**
CHANGE WHEN THE BALLOON IS
EXPOSED TO SUNLIGHT?

Materials
Two blue-colored balloons
Dark closet

Procedure
Inflate each balloon and tie it closed. Place one balloon in a dark closet. Place the second balloon in a window that gets plenty of sunlight.

Compare the color and appearance of each balloon every day for four days.

Observations
Does the color of the balloon in the closet seem to change? Does the color of the balloon placed in the window seem to change? Does the surface of the balloon placed in the window change?

Discussion
In this experiment you should find that the blue color of the balloon placed in the window fades. In contrast, the blue color of the balloon kept in the closet should not fade. You may also find that the surface of the balloon placed in the window becomes chalky.

A balloon is made of rubber molecules. Balloons also contain some dye molecules that give the balloon its color.

The blue color in the balloon placed in the window fades because oxygen molecules in the air react with the blue dye molecules on the surface of the balloon. The oxygen changes the blue dye molecules on the surface of the balloon into other molecules that are colorless

or have very little color. The chalky look on the surface of the balloon is due to the blue dye molecules being changed into other molecules.

Sunlight is needed for the oxygen molecules to react quickly with the blue dye molecules. Sunlight makes the oxygen molecules more reactive. The blue balloon in the closet does not fade, or fades slowly, because it is kept out of the sunlight.

Oxygen molecules can also react with the rubber molecules in the balloon. If the balloon is left in sunlight long enough, the rubber in the balloon looses its strength and tears easily.

Other things to try

Repeat this experiment using different colored balloons. Do all the different colored balloons fade? Do some colored balloons fade less than others?

CAN YOU MAKE BLEACH FROM SALT WATER?   **11**

Materials

One-cup measuring cup	Two pieces of mechanical pencil lead
Tablespoon	Water
Blue food coloring	Small jar (baby food size)
Large jar	Two wires with alligator clips at each end
Salt	Two bowls
6-volt lantern battery	Goggles

Procedure

ASK AN ADULT TO HELP YOU WITH THIS EXPERIMENT. ELECTRICITY CAN BE DANGEROUS. NEVER PUT HOUSE CURRENT (electricity from a wall outlet) IN WATER. YOU SHOULD USE ONLY A 6-VOLT LANTERN BATTERY IN THIS EXPERIMENT. WEAR GOGGLES WHEN YOU DO THIS EXPERIMENT.

Pour two cups of water into the large jar. Add one tablespoon of salt and stir for about thirty seconds to help dissolve the salt. Pour enough salt water from the large jar to fill the small jar.

Clip one end of the first wire to the negative (–) terminal of the battery. Clip one end of the second wire to the positive (+) terminal of the battery. Gently clip the free end of each wire to each piece of mechanical pencil lead.

Place both pieces of pencil lead into the salt water in the small jar. Hold them in place for three minutes. Watch the water for bubbles. DO NOT LET THE ELECTRICITY FLOW THROUGH THE WATER FOR MORE THAN THREE MINUTES. After three minutes, remove the lead from the salt water. Disconnect the wires from the battery.

If there are no bubbles, then you have a loose wire, bad connection, or a dead battery. Check all the wires and connections.

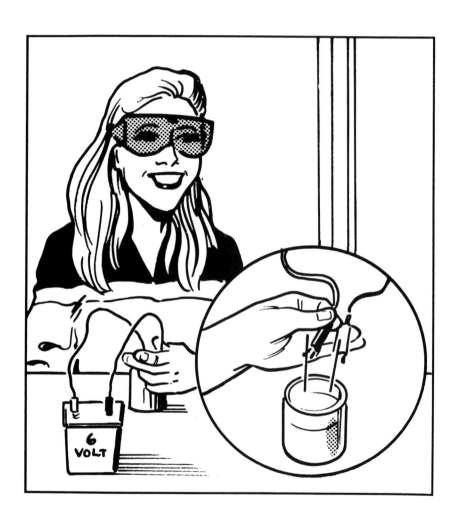

molecules gain this extra energy from light, a message is sent through the attached cells and through the optic nerve to the brain.

The vision process begins when rhodopsin absorbs light. It is the retinal part of rhodopsin that absorbs the light. Retinal can exist in two different forms—twisted and extended (stretched out). Retinal is attached to the opsin in the twisted form.

When light is absorbed, retinal changes to the extended form and separates from the opsin. This triggers the vision process. Gradually, retinal changes back to the twisted form and connects back to the opsin portion. Since this process takes time, we cannot see when we first go from bright light to dim light. We have a time delay because the chemistry going on inside our eyes takes time.

In very dim light, you can detect light and dark but not colors. Colors are detected because the cones are sensitive to three different colors: blue, green, and yellow-red. Other colors of light cause different combinations of these three colors to respond.

In extremely bright light, a person cannot see because there is no retinal left attached to the opsin to absorb the light. All the retinal is in the separated and extended form.

If you do other tests of how your eyes respond to changing amounts of light, remember NEVER STARE AT A BRIGHT LIGHT OR LOOK DIRECTLY AT THE SUN. THIS COULD DAMAGE YOUR EYES.

Other things to try

Repeat this experiment several times. After the light has been on for about thirty seconds and turned off, count until you see the lines. How long does it take before your eyes adjust to the dim light?

Make different color lines on a sheet of white paper. As you dim the lights, observe the page of lines. Are any of the colors easier to see in the dim light?

HOW DO POLAROID™ SUNGLASSES 13 AFFECT SCATTERED LIGHT?

Materials
Polaroid™ sunglasses
Small flashlight
Clear drinking glass
Milk
Water
Measuring spoon
Measuring cup
Dark room (a closet works well)

Procedure
Add one cup of water to the clear drinking glass. Next, add one-quarter teaspoon of milk. Stir the water and milk mixture with a spoon for ten seconds.

Take the glass of milky water, Polaroid™ sunglasses, and flashlight into a room that can be darkened by turning off the lights (a closet works well). Place the glass of milky water on a table or shelf. Turn on the flashlight and shine the light through the glass of milky water. You may need to put the flashlight against the glass.

Look carefully at the glass. You should be able to see the light beam pass through the milky water solution. If you do not see the light beam, add milk (one-quarter teaspoon at a time, then stirring) until you can see the light beam.

While looking at the light beam passing through the milky water, put on the pair of Polaroid™ sunglasses. What do you observe about the light beam? Remove the sunglasses. Now what do you observe about the light beam?

Observations

Is the milky water clear or cloudy? Does the milky water have a slight bluish color?

What happens to the light beam when you put on the sunglasses? What happens when you remove the sunglasses?

Discussion

You see a light beam in the glass of milky water because the light from the flashlight is scattered by particles in the milk. When light is scattered, it goes in many directions. The particles in the milky water that scatter the light consist of fat and protein molecules.

Light from the flashlight is called white light because it contains all the colors of the rainbow. These colors are: violet, indigo, blue, green,

Some colors of light can be scattered more than others. The particles in the milky water cause blue light to be scattered more than the other colors. This is why the milky water appears slightly bluish.

When you look at the glass of milky water while wearing Polaroid™ sunglasses, you should find that you can no longer see the light beam passing through the milky water. When you remove the Polaroid™ sunglasses, the light beam can be seen.

Polaroid™ sunglasses are made to allow light to pass through in mostly an up-and-down direction. Polaroid sunglasses block light that moves mostly in a side-to-side orientation. Ordinary light, like white light from a flashlight, does not have any special direction of orientation.

When the light from the flashlight is scattered by the particles in the milky water, the scattered light is made to travel in a side-to-side orientation. The scattered light is blocked by the Polaroid™ sunglasses because the sunglasses only allow light moving in mostly an up-and-down direction to pass through. You no longer see the light beam passing through the milky water when you wear the Polaroid™ sunglasses.

Polaroid™ sunglasses are effective at reducing glare. Glare is scattered light. Much of the scattered light that makes glare travels in a side-to-side orientation and is blocked by the Polaroid™ sunglasses.

Other things to try

Shine a flashlight onto a shiny countertop or other flat surface to produce a glare. What happens to the glare when you put on the Polaroid™ sunglasses?

CAN YOU MAKE A MAGNET FROM AN IRON NAIL? **14**

Materials

Iron nail (one and a half inches long)
Horseshoe magnet
Small iron nail (a half inch long)

Procedure

Touch the point of the large nail to the point of the smaller nail. Make sure that the small nail is not attracted to the large one. If the nails are attracted to each other, you will need to get two other nails.

Place the large nail across the horseshoe magnet. Leave the nail attached to the magnet for at least twenty-four hours. Do not let the smaller nail come near the magnet. After one day (twenty-four hours), remove the large nail from the magnet.

Touch the point of the large nail to the point of the small nail. Slowly move the large nail and observe the small nail.

You are using a horseshoe magnet in this experiment because it is a strong magnet. You could try this experiment with a smaller, weaker magnet (like one used to hold paper on a refrigerator door). However, you may need to leave the nail on the magnet for a longer time. It may be harder for the nail to change.

Observations

Is the small nail attracted to the large nail? Can you lift the small nail with the large nail?

Discussion

By leaving an iron nail in contact with a strong magnet, you are able to magnetize the nail. After the nail is magnetized, it will act just like a magnet. The magnetized nail should be able to pick up another nail. You may find that the magnet is strongest at the point of the nail.

Electrons may spin in a clockwise or counter-clockwise direction around the positively charged center of an atom (nucleus). If there are more electrons in an atom with a spin in one direction than another, the atom will act like a tiny magnet. These magnetic atoms in iron tend to line up in the same direction as other nearby atoms. This creates magnetic regions called domains.

At first, the magnetic domains in the nail point in all different directions. The iron nail is not magnetic. All the individual magnetic domains cancel each other out.

When the magnet is next to the nail, it attracts the magnetic atoms and causes domains within the nail to line up. When enough of the domains point in the same direction, the nail becomes magnetic. The domains remain locked into position, even after the nail is removed from the magnet. The large nail remains magnetic.

Some types of explosive navy mines attack enemy ships by detecting the magnetic fields of ships. When ships are made, the steel in the ship can become magnetic. The passing magnetic field is a signal to set off the mine.

Other things to try

Place one end of the horseshoe magnet on a nail that is not magnetic. Firmly rub the magnet toward the point of the nail. Repeat this rubbing procedure at least thirty times. Always rub from the head toward the point of the nail. Does the nail become magnetic? Can it pick up another nail?

Sometimes a tool such as a screwdriver may be magnetized by wrapping a wire around the screwdriver and passing a current through the wire to create a magnetic field. Try magnetizing a steel-bladed screwdriver by rubbing it with a horseshoe magnet. Will the screwdriver pick up and hold steel screws?

CAN ELECTRONS MOVING IN A WIRE CAUSE A COMPASS NEEDLE TO MOVE?

Materials
Magnetic compass
Insulated wire about six feet long
6-volt lantern battery

Procedure
Wrap the insulated wire in a tight coil around the magnetic compass. Leave about twelve inches of extra wire at each end that is not wrapped around the compass. Wrap the wire until you have at least ten coils around the compass.

HAVE AN ADULT remove about one inch of insulation from each end of the wire. Set the compass on a flat surface. Connect one end of the wire to the positive (+) terminal of the battery. Observe the needle of the compass.

Turn the compass until the wire wrapping is parallel (in the same direction) to the compass needle. Connect the other end of the wire to the negative (–) terminal of the battery. Observe the compass needle.

Disconnect the wires from the battery. Switch the wires connected to the positive and negative battery terminals. Observe the compass needle.

Observations
What happens to the compass needle when the wires are connected? What happens to the compass needle when the wires are reversed?

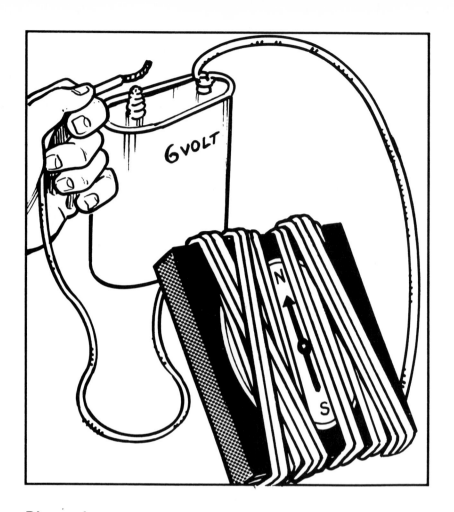

Discussion

The earth's magnetic field causes a compass needle to point north. However, your compass needle changes direction when the wires are connected and current flows.

When both ends of the wire are connected to the battery, the compass needle moves perpendicular to the wire. Two objects are perpendicular if they are at right angles to each other, like a plus sign. When you switch the ends of the wire connected to the battery, the compass needle points in the opposite direction.

A metal is made of charged atoms with some free electrons. These free electrons can move through the metal while the atoms stay in place. Moving electrons carry electricity through the metal.

When you connect both ends of the wire to the battery, you complete a circuit. The circuit is the path that electrons follow. Electrons flow from the negative terminal of the battery through the metal wire, and back to the positive terminal. Moving electrons generate a magnetic field.

The magnetic field makes the compass needle move. When the circuit is broken by removing a wire from the battery, the electron flow stops and the magnetic field is turned off.

In the early part of the nineteenth century, some scientists thought magnetic fields and electric currents might be connected. They thought that a current of electricity flowing through a wire would cause a magnetic needle to line up parallel to the wire.

In 1820, a scientist named Hans Christian Oersted placed a compass needle parallel to a coil of wire. When current flowed through the wire, he was surprised to see the compass needle move to the perpendicular position. He accidentally discovered that a current of electrons moving in a wire causes a perpendicular magnetic field.

At first, other scientists did not believe him. They were certain that the magnetic field would be parallel to the wire. Finally, other scientists accepted the idea that a current in a wire causes a magnetic field perpendicular to the wire.

Other things to try

Slip the coil of wire off the compass. How far can you remove the coil from the compass and still cause the needle to move?

Repeat this experiment with a single coil of wire. Is the magnetic field weaker with fewer coils?

WHAT HAPPENS WHEN A MAGNET 16
DROPS THROUGH A COPPER PIPE?

Materials
Copper pipe (about 5 feet long and having a diameter
    of half an inch)
Magnet (small enough to just fit into the copper pipe
    without touching the sides)
Nail

Procedure

For this experiment you will need a straight piece of copper pipe about 5 feet long (1.5 meters) and having a diameter of half an inch (1.3 cm). Copper pipe can be found at most hardware and building supply stores. Use a nail that is about the same size and weight as the magnet you are going to use in this experiment.

To show that copper is not attracted by a magnet, touch the magnet to the copper pipe. The magnet should not stick to the copper pipe.

Ask a friend to hold the copper pipe straight up and down. You will want to hold the pipe over a carpeted floor or rug so the nail and magnet do not damage the floor. Hold the magnet in one hand and the nail in the other. Insert the nail into the top of the copper pipe, but do not let go of it just yet. Hold the magnet at the same height as the nail. Release the nail and the magnet at the same time. Observe the nail and magnet hitting the floor. Repeat this experiment several times to make sure you obtain consistent results.

Now insert the magnet into the top of the copper pipe. Hold the nail at the same height as the magnet. Release the magnet and nail at the same time. Observe the magnet and nail hitting the floor. Repeat this experiment several times to make sure you obtain consistent results.

Observations

When the nail is dropped through the copper pipe, do the nail and magnet hit the floor at the same time?

When the magnet is dropped through the copper pipe, do the nail and magnet hit the floor at the same time?

Discussion

You should find that when the nail drops through the copper pipe, the nail and magnet hit the floor at the same time. In contrast, when

the magnet drops through the copper pipe, you should find that the nail hits the floor before the magnet. The magnet passes through the copper pipe more slowly than the nail, even though both weigh about the same.

Copper is a good conductor of electricity. The pipe is a good conductor of electricity because it is made of copper. When the magnet drops down the pipe, the magnet's field causes free electrons in the copper pipe to swirl around. The swirling electrons in the copper pipe are called an "induced current." A current is a flow of electrons.

Any time electrons flow through a conductor, a magnetic field is created. The swirling electrons in the copper pipe that are induced by the magnet moving through the pipe create a magnetic field.

Working in the middle of the nineteenth century, German physicist and explorer Heinrich Lenz discovered that induced magnetic fields always oppose the force that creates them. This means that the magnetic field associated with the swirling electrons in the copper pipe opposes or repulses the magnetic field associated with the magnet that is moving through the pipe. Since the magnet that moves through the copper pipe is being opposed by the magnetic field associated with the swirling electrons in the copper pipe, it passes through the copper pipe more slowly than the nail. The nail is not magnetic, so no forces are created in the copper pipe to oppose the nail as it moves down the pipe.

Other things to try

Try this experiment with different magnets. You should find that the stronger the magnet the more slowly it will move through the copper pipe. Try it and see.

CAN YOU DETECT THE IODINE IN   **17**
IODIZED TABLE SALT?

Materials

Iodized table salt

Corn starch

3 percent hydrogen peroxide (available
   at most grocery and drug stores)

Water

Goggles (available in hardware stores)

Measuring cup

Measuring spoons

Two plastic spoons

Tape

Felt pen

Two clear drinking glasses

Procedure

USE ONLY A 3 PERCENT (3%) HYDROGEN PEROXIDE SOLU-TION. CAREFULLY READ THE LABEL ON THE BOTTLE. ASK AN ADULT TO HELP YOU WITH THIS EXPERIMENT. DO NOT GET THIS SOLUTION IN YOUR EYES. WEAR GOGGLES WHEN YOU DO THIS EXPERIMENT.

Place a piece of tape on each glass. Label one glass "water" and the other "hydrogen peroxide." Add one-quarter cup of water to the glass labeled "water." Next, add one-quarter cup of 3 percent hydrogen peroxide to the cup labeled "hydrogen peroxide."

Add two tablespoons of iodized table salt to the glass labeled "water" and stir with a plastic spoon for thirty seconds. Not all the salt will dissolve.

Now add two tablespoons of iodized salt to the glass labeled "hydrogen peroxide" and stir with a plastic spoon for thirty seconds. Again, not all the salt will dissolve.

Place the two glasses beside each other and allow them to sit for two minutes. After this time observe and describe any differences between the two glasses.

Add one-quarter teaspoon of powdered corn starch to each glass. Stir each glass with a spoon for thirty seconds. What changes take place in each glass?

When you are through making your observations, pour the contents of each glass down the kitchen sink and rinse each glass thoroughly with water.

Observations

Is the salt water solution labeled "water" cloudy or clear after stirring? Is the salt water solution labeled "hydrogen peroxide" cloudy or clear after stirring? After sitting for two minutes, is there a color change in one of the glasses? What color forms in one of the glasses when powdered corn starch is added to the glasses?

Discussion

Table salt is the most common seasoning for food. Two kinds of table salt are available in grocery stores. Plain table salt and iodized table salt. Plain table salt is nearly pure sodium chloride (NaCl). Iodized table salt is sodium chloride to which a small amount of potassium iodide (KI) has been added.

Sodium chloride is made of positive sodium ions (Na+) and negative chlorine ions (Cl-). Potassium iodide is made of positive potassium ions (K+) and negative iodine ions (I-). Ions are charged atoms.

Iodine is an essential nutrient for humans. This important nutrient keeps the thyroid gland functioning properly. The thyroid gland is located in the neck and makes a hormone that helps control the growth and activity of the body.

Only a trace amount of iodine is necessary for the proper functioning of the thyroid gland. Many people get enough iodine from the foods they eat. Seafood is particularly rich in iodine.

A deficiency in iodine can cause goiter, which is a swelling of the thyroid gland. To reduce the incidence of goiter, the United States Food and Drug Administration (FDA) approved, in 1924, the addition of small amounts of potassium iodide to table salt. Potassium iodide was the first food supplement approved by the FDA.

In this experiment, you use a chemical test to show that iodized table salt does contain iodide ions. Two steps are involved in the chemical test. In the first step, iodide ions are changed into molecules of iodine by the 3 percent hydrogen peroxide. Iodine molecules consist of two iodine atoms that are tightly bound together.

The yellow or brown color that you should see in the glass labeled "hydrogen peroxide" two minutes after stirring in the iodized table salt is due to the formation of iodine molecules. The contents of the glass labeled "water" should not be colored, since hydrogen peroxide was not present in this glass to change iodide ions into molecules of iodine.

When you add the corn starch to the glass labeled "hydrogen peroxide," you should see a blue color form. Iodine molecules are easy to detect because they combine with starch to give a blue color. No blue color should form in the glass labeled "water" because this glass does not contain iodine molecules—only iodide ions.

Other things to try

What would happen if you use plain table salt (table salt that does not have added potassium iodide) in the experiment? Try it and see.

CAN TEA BE USED TO TEST FOR IRON IN WATER? **18**

Materials

Two clear plastic cups

Sink

Tea bag

Iron supplement pill (such as ferrous gluconate,
   found in grocery or pharmacy stores)

Measuring cup

Spoon

Hot water

Fork

Procedure

Use a measuring cup to add one cup of hot tap water to a clear plastic cup. Place a tea bag in this cup. Dip the tea bag up and down. After about thirty seconds, remove the tea bag. If the tea is too dark to see through, then you need to add more water.

Add one cup of hot tap water to the second plastic cup. Place an iron pill in this cup. Use a spoon or fork to crush the iron pill into small pieces to help the pill dissolve in the water.

Wait about fifteen minutes to allow the iron more time to dissolve in the water. Stir the water. The water with the iron pill may change color due to the dye used in making the pill or from the coating on the pill.

Slowly pour the iron-water from the second cup into the tea in the first cup. Stir the tea as the water containing iron is added.

Observations

What happens to the cup of tea as the water containing iron is added? Do you see a change in color?

Discussion

Tannins (or tannic acid) are naturally occurring molecules found in the leaves, bark, and fruit of some plants. Tannins are found in coffee, tea, and plants such as oak. Dried tea leaves may contain up to one-fourth of their weight in tannins. Tannins contribute to the brisk taste of tea and the color of tea.

You probably observed a dramatic change in the color of your tea. Your tea should change from a light brown to a dark black color. Tea changes color when ions (charged atoms) of iron are added.

One or more molecules can bond with a single metal ion to form what is called a "coordination complex." In this complex, a molecule

called a ligand supplies a pair of electrons and a metal ion accepts these electrons. This sharing of electrons forms a bond that holds them together. In this experiment tannin molecules can bind with iron to form a coordination complex.

Some molecules, such as water, do not absorb or block light. Others strongly block light and give rise to certain colors. The tannin-iron complex absorbs light and appears black.

Tannin molecules produce a bluish-black color or black particles when combined with iron ions. If there is no iron, the tannin-iron complex will not form and no dark color will occur. This color change can be used to check for the presence of iron in a mixture.

In swamps, the water is often very dark or black due to tannin. The tannin gets into the water from the bark and leaves of decaying plants and trees.

Tannin molecules are used in tanning leather. Tanning causes leather to be tougher and more resistant to moisture and decay.

Other things to try

Try repeating this experiment by first making the solution of iron but then doing a series of dilutions. Add one-half cup of iron water to one-half cup of water. Add one-fourth cup of iron to three-fourths cup of water. Add one tablespoon of iron water to one cup of water. In a fourth container place one cup of plain tap water. Next make four cups of identical tea. Now add to each cup of tea one tablespoon from each of the four different cups of iron water. Does the darkness of the tea change with different concentrations of iron?

HOW CAN YOU USE IRON IONS TO **19** TEST FOR HYDROGEN PEROXIDE?

Materials
Large glass jar
Two clear plastic cups
3 percent hydrogen peroxide (available at most grocery and drug stores)
Water
Measuring cup
Pad of steel wool (fine grade)
Vinegar
Goggles (available in hardware stores)

Procedure

ONLY USE A 3 PERCENT (3%) HYDROGEN PEROXIDE SO-LUTION. READ THE LABEL ON THE BOTTLE. DO NOT GET THIS SOLUTION IN YOUR EYES. HAVE AN ADULT HELP YOU WITH THIS EXPERIMENT. WEAR GOGGLES WHEN YOU DO THIS EX-PERIMENT.

Place the pad of fine steel wool in the bottom of the large glass jar. Add enough vinegar to completely cover the steel wool. Let the jar sit undisturbed for about four hours before you continue the experiment.

Pour one-fourth cup of water into the first plastic cup. Pour one-fourth cup of hydrogen peroxide solution into the second plastic cup.

Pour one-fourth cup of liquid (iron acetate solution) from the jar containing steel wool into each of the plastic cups. Observe the colors of the liquids.

When you are finished, pour all the solutions down the drain and wash the jar and cups with soap and water.

Observations

Do you observe any change in the cup of water? Do you observe any change in the cup of hydrogen peroxide?

Discussion

Vinegar is an acid that reacts with the iron in the steel wool. When the steel wool is soaked in the vinegar, some of the iron changes from atoms in the solid into ions (charged atoms) in the liquid. The iron and vinegar solution is called "iron acetate" because it contains iron ions and acetate ions. The iron comes from the steel wool and the acetate comes from the acetic acid.

The iron acetate solution, water, and hydrogen peroxide solution are all colorless liquids. Both the iron acetate solution and the hydrogen peroxide solution are mostly water.

When iron acetate is added to water there is no change in color. However, when the iron acetate is added to hydrogen peroxide there is a dramatic change. You should see two colorless liquids combine to make an orange or reddish-brown liquid. The hydrogen peroxide combines with the iron ions to form an orange colored liquid. This change shows that hydrogen peroxide is present.

Iron ions (charged atoms) can have a positive charge of either +2 or +3. In the iron acetate solution, the iron atoms have a charge of +2. The peroxide causes the iron to change from a +2 ion to a +3 ion. This change in the charge of the iron is a process called oxidation. Hydrogen peroxide causes the iron to be oxidized.

Hydrogen peroxide solution is mostly water, but it contains some hydrogen peroxide. A hydrogen peroxide molecule contains two oxygen atoms and two hydrogen atoms. Hydrogen peroxide molecules can break apart and recombine to form oxygen molecules and

water molecules or hydroxide (OH-) ions. You may see tiny bubbles of oxygen gas form in the cup with the orange liquid.

The orange color is caused by iron +3 ions combining with hydroxide ions and water to form iron hydroxide or hydrated iron oxide (tiny particles of rust). These particles have an orange or reddish-brown color.

Other things to try

Dilute the 3 percent hydrogen peroxide solution by one-half. Repeat this experiment, using this solution and the regular 3 percent hydrogen peroxide. Can you tell a difference in the amount of hydrogen peroxide by the darkness of the color formed? Does the cup with the weaker hydrogen peroxide give a lighter color solution?

CAN TWO LIQUIDS BE COMBINED TO GIVE SOLID PARTICLES?   **20**

Materials
Large glass jar
Small glass jar
Water
Pad of steel wool (fine grade)
Vinegar
Ammonia (cleaning solution)
Goggles (available in hardware stores)
Measuring cup

Procedure
ASK AN ADULT TO HELP YOU WITH THIS EXPERIMENT. DO NOT GET AMMONIA ON YOUR SKIN OR IN YOUR EYES. WEAR GOGGLES WHEN AMMONIA IS USED.

Spread out the pad of fine steel wool and place it in the bottom of the large glass jar. Add enough vinegar to completely cover the steel wool. Cover the jar and let the jar sit overnight to form an iron and vinegar solution.

Pour about one-eighth cup of iron and vinegar solution (the steel wool should remain in the large jar) from the large jar into the small glass jar. Have an adult pour approximately the same amount of ammonia into the small glass jar. Have an adult return the bottle of ammonia to a safe place.

When you are finished with your experiments, pour all the solutions down the drain and wash the jars with soap and water.

Observations

What happens when these liquids are combined? What changes do you observe when ammonia is added to the iron and vinegar solution?

Discussion

When the iron is soaked in the vinegar overnight, it causes a chemical reaction that causes some of the iron to go from the solid into the liquid as ions (charged atoms). The vinegar is an acid that reacts with the iron in the steel wool. The iron and vinegar solution is called iron acetate. Iron acetate contains iron ions.

The ammonia solution is a base. A base contains hydroxide ions (OH-). A hydroxide ion is made of a hydrogen atom, oxygen atom, and an extra electron.

Neither the iron acetate nor the ammonia solution contains any solids. Both of these solutions are clear liquids. However, when you combine them, you should see a dramatic change. When you combine these liquids, you should see solid bluish-green particles. Two liquids have combined to make solid particles.

The iron ions can have a positive charge of either +2 or +3. Hydroxide ions have a negative charge of -1. Some combinations of positive and negative ions can form solid particles.

Solid particles formed in solution are called a "precipitate." Small solid particles may float in this solution, but larger particles settle to the bottom. Do the solid particles you formed settle to the bottom of the jar?

The bluish-green particles formed in this experiment are a combination of iron and hydroxide ions. Water molecules may also be a part of the solid precipitate. In this experiment, each solution contributed ions toward the final product. The solid could not form until both liquids were mixed together.

Other things to try

Repeat this experiment using one-fourth cup of iron and vinegar solution. Have an adult add ammonia very slowly. What is the minimum amount of ammonia that can be added before solid particles form.

Take your original solution containing the bluish-green solid particles, place it in a safe place and leave it for several hours. What happens to the color of the precipitate? You may find that the particles gradually change to a reddish-brown color. The iron may change to an iron oxide compound with attached water molecules. When iron oxide forms, the color changes.

WHAT HAPPENS WHEN GRAPES ARE PLACED IN WATER AND SUGAR WATER? **21**

Materials
Two identical grapes (same size)
Water
Sugar
Tablespoon
Measuring cup
Two plastic cups
Permanent marker

Procedure
Add one cup of water to the first plastic cup. Mark this cup with a "W." Add one cup of water to the second plastic cup. Add six table-spoons of sugar to this cup. Stir to try to get all the sugar to dissolve into the water.

You will need two grapes that are the same size. Add one grape to each cup. Set the cups where they can remain undisturbed for one week. Observe the grapes in the cups every other day for about a week.

After a week remove the two grapes. Look carefully at each grape. Compare the two grapes.

Observations
What happens to the grapes?

Discussion
You should observe that the grape left in the water is larger than the grape left in the sugar water. The skin of the first grape (from the water) may have cracked because the grape has swollen.

Why would one grape become larger than the other? The change in the size of the grapes is because of osmosis.

The outer coating or layer of a cell or larger object is called a membrane. The outer skin or peel of a grape acts like a membrane. This outer layer allows water to pass into or out of the grape. For water to move through a membrane there must be some force pushing it. One force that pushes water through membranes is called "osmotic pressure."

Molecules of water move from the side of the membrane with less sugar to the side with more sugar. The molecules of water move because of a difference in the concentration of the sugar inside and

outside the grape. When molecules of water move through a membrane because of a difference in concentration, the process is called "osmosis."

In the plain water cup (labeled W), the water is more dilute than the sugar and water mixture inside the grape. Water molecules move through the membrane (skin) of the grape and into the grape. This additional water makes the grape swell and become larger.

In the sugar water cup, the sugar water is about the same concentration as the water and natural sugars in the grape. In the sugar water, the grape does not become larger. However, in very concentrated solutions of sugar water, the grape could shrink. If water leaves the grape, it becomes smaller and wrinkled.

When IV (intravenous) fluids are given to a patient in a hospital, the concentration of the fluid must not be too great or too little. If the concentration of the IV fluid is too great, it could cause the person's red blood cells to shrink. If the concentration of the IV fluid is too little, it could cause the person's red blood cells to get larger. Osmosis is important in the cells of our body.

Other things to try

Repeat this experiment using liquid from a can of regular cola and from a can of diet cola. Place a grape in each type of cola. The regular cola contains sugar. The diet cola contains no sugar. The regular cola is more concentrated than the diet cola. What do you predict will happen? What do you observe?

CAN FREEZING TEMPERATURES HARM PLANTS?   **22**

Materials
Two fresh lettuce leaves
Refrigerator with freezer
Plate

Procedure
Place one fresh lettuce leaf in a freezer. Place the other leaf in a refrigerator and leave them overnight.

Remove both pieces of lettuce and place them on a plate. Observe both lettuce leaves for several minutes as they warm to room temperature. Feel both leaves and compare their shape.

Observations
Do the two lettuce leaves look the same when you first remove them from refrigerator and freezer? Does the green color in the lettuce leaves change when they warm to room temperature?

What happens to the shape and texture of the lettuce leaves when they warm to room temperature? Can you see a watery liquid leaking from the surface of one of the lettuce leaves after both leaves warm to room temperature?

Discussion
Like all living things, plants are made of individual cells. Cells are the basic building blocks of living things. Most cells are extremely small and can only be seen with a microscope. If you could examine a lettuce leaf under a microscope, you would see many cells packed tightly together.

Surrounding plant cells is a cell wall. The cell wall is rigid and gives strength to the cell. The inside of a plant cell contains mostly water and materials necessary for the cell to live and grow.

Freezing can damage plant cells. When plant tissue freezes, water inside the plant cells making up the tissue can change to ice crystals. These ice crystals can puncture the cell wall. When the plant tissue thaws, water inside the punctured cells leaks out of the cell wall. This loss of water from the plant cells causes the plant tissue to wilt and become limp.

When you first removed the frozen lettuce leaf from the freezer, it should have looked like the lettuce leaf stored in the refrigerator.

However, after the frozen lettuce leaf thawed, you should have noticed that it became wilted and slightly dark in color.

You may have noticed the appearance of water on the outside of the thawed lettuce leaf. The wilting and dark color is due to the cell walls being punctured when ice crystals formed in the cells of the lettuce leaf during freezing. The water appearing on the outside of the lettuce is what leaked from the damaged cells.

Frozen vegetables are sold in the frozen food section of grocery stores. Companies that prepare frozen foods try to avoid damaging the cell walls of the vegetables during freezing. They freeze the vegetables very quickly and at a very low temperature. Quick freezing keeps the developing ice crystals in the cells of the vegetables small. Small ice crystals are less likely to damage cell walls.

Other things to try

Repeat this experiment with other leafy vegetables such as cabbage, kale, mustard greens, and collards. Are some leafy vegetables less damaged by freezing than others?

Repeat this experiment with other vegetables and fruits such as broccoli, green peppers, mushrooms, apples, and pears. What do you observe?

WHAT HAPPENS TO SPINACH WHEN **23** IT IS FIRST PLACED IN HOT WATER?

Materials

Fresh spinach leaves

Saucepan

Water

Stove

Measuring cup

Slotted spoon (spoon with holes)

Paper towel

Procedure

ASK AN ADULT TO HELP YOU WITH THIS EXPERIMENT. DO NOT USE THE STOVE BY YOURSELF.

Add one cup of water to a saucepan. Have an adult heat the pan of water on the stove until the water boils. Turn off the burner that was used.

Using a slotted spoon, carefully lower a spinach leaf into the hot water. After fifteen seconds, remove the spinach leaf from the hot water and place it on a paper towel to drain. Place a fresh spinach leaf next to the heated spinach leaf. Compare the color of the spinach leaves.

Observations

When you first place the spinach leaf in the hot water, does the color change? What happens to the color of the spinach leaf when you remove it from the water and place it on the paper towel?

Discussion

Contained within the leaves of green plants are many tiny gas bubbles. These tiny gas bubbles are found in small openings covering the surface of green leaves. These small openings are called "stomata." The stomata of leaves can only be seen with a microscope.

72

Stomata are necessary for green plants to carry out photosynthesis. Photosynthesis is the process by which green plants capture and store energy from the sun. During photosynthesis, green plants use sunlight to change carbon dioxide gas and water into energy-rich chemical substances. Oxygen gas is also made during photosynthesis.

Leaves take in carbon dioxide gas from the atmosphere through their stomata during photosynthesis. The oxygen gas made by the leaves is also released through the stomata. There is always some gas in the stomata of leaves.

You should find that when you first add the fresh spinach leaf to the hot water, the green color of the leaf becomes brighter. When you add the leaf to the hot water, the leaf warms up. When the gas bubbles in the stomata of the leaf warm up, they expand. A gas always tries to expand when it is heated.

When the gas inside the stomata expands, the stomata expands and becomes larger. More light passes through a leaf when the stomata become larger. Since more light passes through the leaf when the stomata are larger, the leaf appears brighter.

Other things to try

Repeat this experiment, but leave the spinach leaf in the hot water for five minutes. What happens to the color of the spinach leaf? You may find that the spinach leaf has lost its green color and is now brownish-green.

Repeat this experiment with other green, leafy vegetables such as cabbage, turnip greens, and collards.

CAN GREEN VEGETABLES BECOME 24 BROWN WHEN THEY ARE COOKED?

Materials
Fresh spinach leaves
Two small saucepans
Water
Vinegar
Measuring cup
Measuring spoons
Spoon for stirring
Stove
Clock or watch
Tape

Procedure
ASK AN ADULT TO HELP YOU WITH THIS EXPERIMENT. DO NOT USE THE STOVE BY YOURSELF.

Add one cup of water to each saucepan. Place three spinach leaves in each pan. Stir each pan with a spoon.

To identify one of the pans, place a small piece of tape on the handle of one of the saucepans. Add one tablespoon of vinegar to this pan. Stir with a spoon to mix the vinegar with the water and spinach leaves.

Have an adult heat both pans on the stove using medium-high heat. Reduce the heat to a lower setting when the water in each pan begins to boil. Simmer the contents of each pan for five minutes. Turn off the stove. Leave the pans on the stove. The pans will be hot and should not be touched.

Compare the color of the spinach leaves in each pan.

Allow each pan to cool for one hour. Compare the color of the spinach leaves in each pan after one hour.

Observations

What is the color of the spinach leaves in the pan containing just water? What is the color of the spinach leaves in the pan containing water and vinegar?

What color are the spinach leaves in each pan after cooling for one hour?

Discussion

Spinach, like all green plants, contains chlorophyll. Chlorophyll is a pigment which gives green plants their color. Green plants use chlorophyll to capture and store energy from the sun in a process called "photosynthesis."

Chlorophyll is a large, complex molecule. Near the center of the molecule is a cavity. The chlorophyll molecule holds a positively charged magnesium atom (ion, Mg+2) in this cavity. This magnesium ion is necessary for the chlorophyll molecule to carry out photosynthesis. This magnesium ion gives the chlorophyll molecule a green color.

The chlorophyll molecule does not hold the magnesium ion tightly in its cavity. Since the magnesium ion is not held tightly, it can be easily removed from the chlorophyll molecule. When the magnesium ion is removed from a chlorophyll molecule, the color of the chlorophyll molecule changes from green to brownish-green.

In this experiment, you use vinegar and heat to remove the magnesium ions from the cavities of the chlorophyll molecules in spinach leaves. You can tell when you remove the magnesium ions from the chlorophyll molecules in the spinach because the spinach turns to a brownish-green color.

Vinegar is an acid. An acid is a source of positive hydrogen ions (H+). When you heat the spinach leaves in water containing vinegar, the heat causes the magnesium ions to break away from the chloro-phyll molecules. As the magnesium ions move away from the cavities of the chlorophyll molecules, H+ ions from the acid in vinegar move into the cavities.

The H+ ions are held more tightly in the cavities of chlorophyll molecules than magnesium ions. This keeps the magnesium ions from returning to the cavities of the chlorophyll molecules as the spinach leaves cool. This is why the spinach leaves that were heated with vinegar remained brownish-green after cooling for one hour.

Other things to try

Repeat this experiment with other green vegetables such as green beans, turnip greens, kale, collards, broccoli, cabbage, and celery. Do some green vegetables turn less brown than others when heated in water containing vinegar?

CAN AN ONION BRING TEARS TO YOUR EYES?

Materials

Unpeeled onion
Knife
Plate

Procedure

ASK AN ADULT TO HELP YOU WITH THIS EXPERIMENT. DO NOT USE A KNIFE BY YOURSELF.

Sniff the outside of an unpeeled onion.

Ask an adult to slice the onion in half. Bring one of the onion halves near your nose. Sniff the cut surface of the onion for about ten seconds.

Observations

Does the unpeeled onion have a smell? Does the cut surface of the onion have a smell? Does the cut onion make your eyes water?

Discussion

You may have found in this experiment that when you sniffed the cut surface of an onion, tears came to your eyes. You may have also noticed the onion gave off a sharp, onion odor. In contrast, the unpeeled onion had little, if any, odor.

For most people, chopping onions brings tears to their eyes. When an onion is cut, onion cells on the cut surface are torn open and their contents are released. A chemical reaction in the exposed cell fluid occurs to make a molecule that contains sulfur atoms. This sulfur-containing molecule is made when an onion cell is cut. These molecules quickly escape into the air. The sharp onion smell you notice on the surface of a cut onion is caused by these molecules.

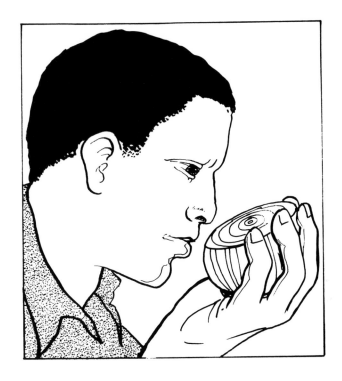

When this sulfur-containing molecule gets into your eyes, it mixes with the water in your eyes. A chemical reaction occurs between the water in your eye and the sulfur-containing compound to make acid molecules. These acid molecules irritate your eyes. Your eyes produce large amounts of tears to wash out the acids.

Other things to try

Rinse one of the cut halves of onion under running cold water for ten seconds. Compare the smell of the washed onion half with the half that was not washed. Is the smell coming from the washed onion half less than the smell coming from the unwashed onion half?

The sulfur-containing compound, made when an onion is cut, easily dissolves in water. To keep from crying when cutting onions, some people cut their onions under running water.

HOW DOES HOT WATER CHANGE DIFFERENT PLASTICS? **26**

Materials
Clear plastic cup with a PETE code on the bottom
Clear plastic cup with a PS code on the bottom
Water
Kettle
Stove burner
Sink

Procedure
ASK AN ADULT TO HELP YOU WITH THIS EXPERIMENT. DO NOT USE A STOVE OR BOILING HOT WATER BY YOURSELF.

Set the clear PETE cup and the clear PS cup in the sink. The PETE cup should have the number "1" inside a triangle and the letters "PETE" on the bottom of the cup. The PS cup should have the number "6" inside a triangle and the letters "PS" on the bottom of the cup.

Partially fill a kettle with water. Place the kettle on a stove burner and set the burner on a high setting. Leave the kettle on the stove until the water is boiling. Turn off the burner. HAVE AN ADULT carefully pour hot water from the kettle to fill each of the cups in the sink.

BE CAREFUL, BOILING WATER IS VERY HOT AND CAN BURN.

Wait several minutes to allow the water to cool before you touch the cups. After the water is cooled, examine each of the cups.

Observations
What happens to each of the cups? Are there any changes in the PETE cup? Are there any changes in the PS cup?

Discussion

Codes are placed on the bottom of plastics to identify their types. These codes are helpful when we recycle plastics. The 1-PETE code stands for a type of plastic called "polyethylene terephthalate." The 6-PS code stands for a type a plastic called "polystyrene."

You probably observed that the PS cup was not affected by the hot water. However, the PETE cup was changed by the hot water. The cup made of the PETE plastic may have shrunk in size or changed shape. Boiling hot water will soften the PETE plastic, but not the PS plastic. While it is soft, the shape of the PETE plastic cup can change.

The "glass transition temperature" is a temperature at which the properties of a polymer can change. Above the glass transition temperature, a plastic is soft and flexible. Below the glass transition temperature, a plastic is stiff and rigid. As you approach the glass transition temperature, a polymer may become softer and more flexible.

At higher temperatures, a plastic may become more flexible and stretchy like a rubber band. At lower temperatures, plastics like PS and PETE becomes stiffer and more rigid. At a high enough temperature, these plastics will melt to a liquid and can be poured into a mold and formed into any desired shape or object.

The glass transition temperature of polystyrene (PS) is much higher than that of polyethylene terephthalate (PETE). The boiling water is hot enough to soften the PETE cup but not hot enough to soften the PS cup. It may be easier to recycle PETE because scrap plastic can be melted and formed into new products at a lower temperature.

Other things to try

Repeat this experiment using hot tap water. Is this water hot enough to cause a change in either of the cups?

Does the community you live in collect plastics for recycling? If they do, find out what types of plastics are recycled. Is PETE collected for recycling? Is PS collected for recycling? Are other plastics collected?

DOES A PLASTIC BAG GET STRONGER AS YOU STRETCH IT?

27

Materials

Clear plastic bag (use a large Ziploc® storage bag, not a small
  sandwich bag)

Procedure

Firmly grab the top and bottom of the clear, plastic storage bag
and pull. As you stretch the bag, feel how hard you pull. Continue to
pull on the bag until it breaks. Repeat this several times with other
plastic bags of the same type.

If the bag breaks too easily, you may need to get a larger bag
made with thicker sheets of plastic. If the bag is too hard to stretch,
you may need to get someone to help you stretch it.

Observations

How does the bag feel as you first start to pull on it? Does the bag
stretch in the direction you are pulling? As you continue to pull, does
the bag get harder or easier to pull apart?

Discussion

Clear plastic sandwich bags are usually made of polyethylene.
Polyethylene is a type of polymer. Polymer molecules are long molecules that are made of many smaller units that are repeated over and
over.

Polyethylene is made of a smaller molecule called ethylene (also
called ethene). Since the polymer is made of many ethylene molecules
linked together, it is called polyethylene. The prefix "poly" means many.

Billions and billions of pounds of polyethylene are made and used
around the world. Polyethylene is made by combining ethylene molecules. The process of making a polymer is called "polymerization."

As you first pull on the plastic bag, you probably find that the bag is easy to stretch. As you pull more, you should find that it is harder and harder to pull the bag farther apart. It becomes more difficult to stretch the bag. However, if you pull hard enough, the bag will break.

Imagine many strings of beads all tangled together. As you first pull on the strings, they begin to untangle and line up. As you continue to pull them apart, the strings of beads line up in long straight rows next to each other.

At first it would be easy to stretch out the strings of beads because they are tangled together. Once the long strings of beads are lined up,

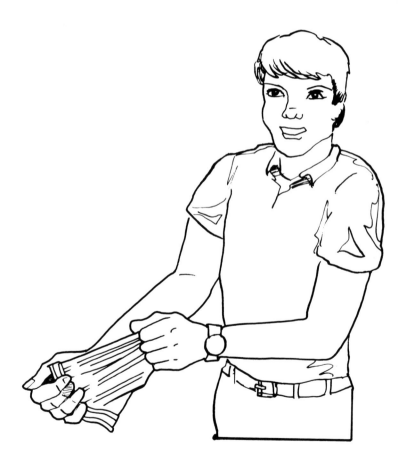

it would become very difficult to stretch the strings any more. However, if you pull hard enough, the strings of beads will break apart.

We can think of the polyethylene molecules like miniature strings of beads. Imagine the ethylene units lined up one after another—like beads attached together to make a long string of beads.

The polymer molecules are initially tangled together, and as you pull, you straighten them out. Pulling the bag is easy at first. As the polymer molecules move apart, the bag stretches. When the polyethylene molecules are lined up side by side, it is difficult to stretch the bag any further. However, if you pull hard enough, the bag breaks, and the long chains of polymers are broken.

Other things to try

Repeat this experiment, pulling very slowly on a plastic bag. Repeat it again, but this time pull the bag apart very rapidly. Do you notice any difference in how hard it is to stretch or break the bag when you pull slow or fast?

Stretch a plastic bag and let go. Now stretch a rubber band and let go. In what ways are they similar? In what ways are they different?

You probably find that the rubber band snaps back, while the polyethylene bag remains stretched when released.

Rubber bands are made of long chains of molecules that are linked together by sulfur atoms. These sulfur links cause the rubber molecules to snap back into position after they have been stretched out. These sulfur links are not present in natural rubber, but must be added by a chemical process called "vulcanization" in which a sulfur and rubber mixture is heated. Vulcanization was discovered in 1839 by Charles Goodyear.

HOW DOES HEAT AFFECT WRINKLES IN CLOTHING?

28

Materials
Steam iron
Wrinkled cotton cloth (the cotton cloth must be 100 percent
   cotton—a cotton T-shirt works well)
Water
Ironing board

Procedure
ASK AN ADULT TO HELP YOU WITH THIS EXPERIMENT. HAVE THE ADULT USE THE HOT IRON WHILE YOU OBSERVE THE CLOTH. DO NOT USE A HOT IRON BY YOURSELF.

Add water to the iron. Turn the steam setting on the iron to off. Plug in the iron and set the temperature to low (delicate). When the iron becomes ready, iron a small area on a piece of wrinkled cotton cloth. Observe any changes in the wrinkled cloth.

Now set the temperature of the iron to high (cotton). Leave the steam off. When the iron is ready, iron a small area on the piece of wrinkled cotton cloth. Observe any changes in the wrinkled cloth.

Leave the temperature setting on high and turn on the steam setting on the iron. Iron a small area on the wrinkled cotton cloth. Observe any changes in the wrinkled cloth.

When you are done, make sure to turn off and unplug the iron.

Observations
Do the wrinkles disappear when you iron the cotton cloth at a low temperature setting? Do the wrinkles disappear when you iron the cotton cloth at a high temperature setting? Does ironing on a high temperature setting and with steam make the ironing easier?

Discussion

Cotton is made of tiny fibers which are spun into thread. Cotton thread is used to make cloth.

Cotton fibers come from cotton plants. Each cotton fiber contains a large number of polymer molecules. Polymers are large, chain-like molecules made by linking together smaller molecules. The smaller molecules linked together in cotton are glucose molecules. Glucose is a simple sugar made during photosynthesis.

The polymer chains in the cotton fibers are twisted and coiled around each other—like cooked spaghetti. Normally, the polymer chains are not free to move around. Instead, they are locked into place.

When polymer chains are heated to a specific temperature, they become more free to move. The temperature at which polymer molecules become more free to move is called the "glass transition temperature." Different polymers can have different glass transition temperatures.

In this experiment, you should have found that the wrinkles remained in the cotton cloth after ironing at a low temperature setting. You should have found the wrinkles were removed from the cloth when it was ironed at a high temperature setting.

The wrinkles were not removed from the cloth at a low temperature setting because the iron was not hot enough to heat the polymer chains in the cotton fibers to their glass transition temperature. The polymer chains in the cotton fibers were not free to move around and be made flat by the smooth surface of the iron.

The wrinkles were removed from the cloth at a high temperature setting because the iron heated the polymer chains in the cotton fibers to their glass transition temperature. The more freely moving polymer chains were then made flat by the smooth surface of the iron. When the iron was removed from the cotton cloth, the polymer chains in the cotton fibers cooled below their glass transition temperature and became locked into their new position.

You should have found ironing on a high temperature setting and with the steam turned on makes using the iron much easier and faster. The steam penetrates the cotton fibers and lubricates the polymer chains, allowing them to move more freely over each other.

Other things to try

Examine the settings on your iron. You may see four or more settings. These settings are low (delicate), medium (permanent press), high (cotton), and maximum. These different temperature settings are used with different fabrics. For example, low is used for silk and rayon fabrics. The polymers in these fabrics have a low glass transition temperature. A medium temperature setting is used for permanent press. Permanent press fabrics are usually made from polyester fibers. Polyester has a lower glass transition temperature than cotton. The maximum temperature setting is used with fabrics made of polymers with high glass transition temperatures. Linen is one such fabric.

IS HAIR MORE ELASTIC WHEN IT IS WET?

29

Materials

Two strands of dry, long hair (at least six inches long)
Bowl
Warm water

Procedure

Place one of the strands of long hair in the bowl containing warm water. Push the hair down into the water. Leave the hair in warm water for fifteen minutes. Keep the second strand of hair dry.

Remove the strand of hair from the warm water. While holding the ends of the strand of hair (one in each hand) pull the hair to stretch it. Allow the strand of hair to relax, and then stretch it again.

Now hold the ends of the strand of dry hair in each hand. Pull the dry hair to stretch it.

Observations

Does the wet hair or the dry hair stretch more easily? Which hair stretches longer?

Discussion

Hair is made of protein. Proteins are large molecules made by living organisms. Protein molecules are made by joining smaller molecules together in long chains. The smaller molecules which are joined together to make proteins are called "amino acids."

A strand of hair is made of a large number of bundles of protein molecules. Each bundle contains many protein molecules which are wrapped around each other in a rope-like fashion. The bundles of protein molecules in a strand of hair are mostly straight and long. The bundles resemble a tightly held handful of uncooked spaghetti.

In this experiment you should have found that the strand of wet hair is easier to stretch than the strand of dry hair. The strand of wet hair should stretch longer than the strand of dry hair.

Hair stretches because the bundles of protein molecules which are next to each other in a strand of hair can slide over each other.

When hair becomes wet, water penetrates into the strand of hair and surrounds the bundles of protein molecules. The water around the bundles acts like a lubricant and allows the bundles to slide by each other more easily. This is why wet hair stretches more easily than dry hair.

Hair made wet with warm water can be stretched to over twice its length.

Other things to try

Allow the wet strand of hair to dry for several hours. Pull on the hair to stretch it. Does it still stretch easily?

Do you think hair is more elastic (stretchy) on rainy or humid days? How can you find out?

CAN HEAT CHANGE SOME LARGE MOLECULES?

30

Materials

Two pieces of heat-shrinkable tubing (available in the electrical
     section of most hardware stores)
Oven
Piece of aluminum foil
Two oven mitts

Procedure

ASK AN ADULT TO HELP YOU WITH THIS EXPERIMENT. DO
NOT USE THE OVEN BY YOURSELF.

Turn the oven on and set its temperature to 300°F (150°C). Wait
five minutes for the oven to heat up.

Feel a piece of heat-shrinkable tubing. Bend the piece of heat-
shrinkable tubing back and forth.

Place a piece of heat-shrinkable tubing on the piece of aluminum
foil. When the oven has heated up, have an adult place the aluminum
foil and the tubing on a rack in the oven. After two minutes, have an
adult remove the aluminum foil and tubing using an oven mitt. Turn off
the oven.

Let the tubing cool for five minutes. With the oven mitts on, feel
the piece of tubing that was heated. Bend it back and forth. Compare
the wall thickness of the tubing that was not heated with the tubing
that was heated.

Observations

Before being heated, is the heat-shrinkable tubing soft and easy
to bend back and forth? After heating, is the tubing softer or stiffer?
Which piece of tubing has thicker walls?

Discussion

Heat-shrinkable tubing is made of polymer molecules. Polymer molecules are made of thousands of smaller molecules. The smaller molecules are connected together in a chain to make long polymer molecules.

The polymer chains in heat-shrinkable tubing are twisted and tangled around each other—like a bowl of cooked spaghetti. At room temperature, the tangled polymer chains are not able to move freely. Instead, they are locked into place. This makes the tubing rigid and gives it shape.

The polymer chains in the heat-shrinkable tubing remain locked in place until the tubing is heated to a specific temperature. This temperature is called the "glass transition temperature." At the glass transition temperature, the polymer chains become more free to move.

Heat-shrinkable tubing is made by heating special tubing with a small diameter and thick walls. When the tubing reaches the glass transition temperature, it is stretched in a machine to a larger diameter. While still stretched, the tubing is allowed to cool to room temperature. When cool, the tubing remains stretched because the polymer chains are locked into a new position.

In this experiment you should have found that the piece of tubing got smaller after being in the hot oven. The tubing shrank because it was heated above the glass transition temperature of the polymer in the tubing. You should have also noticed that the shrunk tubing has thicker walls and is more rigid than the piece of tubing that was not heated.

Heat-shrinkable polymers are used in shrink packaging—especially in the food industry. Foods, such as lettuce and meat, are often packaged in plastic film that is heat shrunk to give a tight seal.

Other things to try

What should happen to a piece of heat-shrinkable tubing heated for two minutes in an oven set at 200°F (90°C)? With an adult's help, repeat this experiment at this lower temperature. What do you observe?

COMPLETE LIST OF MATERIALS
USED IN THESE EXPERIMENTS

Air pressure gauge
aluminum foil
ammonia

Bicycle tire
bicycle tire pump (push-type, not
    electric)
blue balloons
blue food coloring
bowls, small- and medium-sized

Clear plastic cup (PETE code on
    bottom)
clear plastic cup (PS code on bottom)
clock
coin
cola, diet and regular
cooking oil
copper pipe
corn starch
corn syrup
cotton cloth
countertop

Drinking glass, clear

Flashlight, small
fork

Goggles
grapes
graphite lubricant

Hair, two long strands
heat-shrinkable tubing
horseshoe magnet
hydrogen peroxide (3%)

Ice cubes
insulated wire
iron nails
iron supplement pills
ironing board

Jars, small- and large-sized

Kettle
knife

Lantern battery, 6-volt
lettuce leaves

Magnet, small
magnetic compass
markers (red, blue, and black)
measuring cups
measuring spoons
mechanical pencil lead (two pieces)
milk

Notebook paper

Onion, unpeeled
oven mitt
oven with range top

Paper
paper clips
paper towels
pen
permanent marker
plastic cups
plates
portable radio

Refrigerator freezer
room with light switch

Salt
saucepans
sink
slotted spoon
spinach leaves
spoon
spoons, two small metal
steam iron
steel wool pads
string (four feet long)
sugar
sunglasses, Polaroid™

Tablespoon
tape
tea bag
thermometer, outdoor household

Vinegar

Watch
water
wires with alligator clips at each end

Ziploc® storage bag, large

INDEX